Annapolis
MARYLAND

A PHOTOGRAPHIC PORTRAIT

PHOTOGRAPHY BY LISA MASSON

NARRATIVE BY PATRICIA DEMPSEY

TWIN LIGHTS PUBLISHERS | ROCKPORT, MASSACHUSETTS

Copyright © 2016 by
Twin Lights Publishers, Inc.

All rights reserved. No part of this book may be reproduced in any form without written permission of the copyright owners. All images in this book have been reproduced with the knowledge and prior consent of the artists concerned and no responsibility is accepted by producer, publisher, or printer for any infringement of copyright or otherwise, arising from the contents of this publication. Every effort has been made to ensure that credits accurately comply with information supplied.

First published in the
United States of America by:

Twin Lights Publishers, Inc.
Rockport, Massachusetts 01966
Telephone: (978) 546-7398
www.twinlightspub.com

ISBN: 978-1-934907-44-3

10 9 8 7 6 5 4 3 2 1

(opposite)
Aerial Bridges

(frontispiece)
Back Creek Annapolis Sailing School

(jacket front)
City Dock

(jacket back)
Schooner Races and State House

Book design by:
SYP Design & Production, Inc.
www.sypdesign.com

Printed in China

Where else but in Annapolis can one hail a water taxi and dine with a panoramic sunset dipping behind colonial waterfront buildings and a spectacular State House dome? Compelling photos and narrative reveal what locals already know: this is an intriguing, vibrant place, where residents go about their lives amidst living history in the original city plan, circa 1695, of circles and radiating streets. A short walk from City Dock is a town of beautiful contrasts: elegant Georgian mansions and rows of colorful doors adorned with fresh flowers neighbor modern coffee shops, B&Bs, nautical enterprises, and the U.S. Naval Academy. Sailors breeze past wooden sandbaggers and luxury yachts on the harbor. Shipping, oyster packing, boatbuilding, and sailing are part of Annapolis' proud maritime culture, celebrated today with everything from Schooner races and lighthouse tours, to international sailing championships.

Annapolis, Maryland's capital, has long been a lively political and social hub. Prosperous merchants built elaborate homes for entertaining and the historic district, declared a National Historic Landmark in 1965, has more original 18th-century structures intact than any other city in America. For more than 300 years Annapolitans have opened their doors with Chesapeake hospitality. The city hosts world-class sail and powerboat shows, races and regattas, and a wide array of cultural and recreational events.

Annapolis: A Photographic Portrait is an insider's glimpse, from the bow of a skiff, strolling wooden piers, brick-lined streets, to gardens and mansions, and celebrates the character and beauty of this remarkable city.

Sandbagger Twins

Wooden sandbagger twins, *Bull* and *Bear*, catch the morning light at the National Sailing Hall of Fame pier. Popular in the 19th century, sandbagger sloops used sandbags as ballast to help trim their vessels. The twins race in classic boat regattas in Annapolis.

Ego Alley (top)

This waterway earned its local nickname for the many boaters who enjoy being seen as they cruise into port. Once lined with Chesapeake workboats, today the harbor's maritime use is geared to pleasure craft and a daily parade of luxurious yachts, sailboats, skiffs, kayaks, and even paddle boarders.

Market House City Dock (bottom)

Housing a variety of merchants, the Annapolis Market House is an indoor market space offering treats that range from delectable Maryland crab cakes, to smoothies, to sandwiches, and more. Serving the community since 1788, it's the perfect place to grab a bite to eat, sit on the dock, and enjoy the view.

Kunte Kinte Alex Haley Memorial
(above and right)

Located at City Dock, this memorial commemorates the place where Kunte Kinte, arrived as a slave at the port city aboard the *Lord Ligonier* in 1767, as told in Alex Haley's book, *Roots*. Ed Dwight's sculpture depicts Haley reading to children of different ethnicities.

City Dock Panorama (top)

St. Mary's and St. Anne's churches and the State House are prominent skyline features. Seen from Eastport, their spires and dome are a historic backdrop to the changing commerce at City Dock: From tea and tobacco trading in colonial times, oyster and fisheries harvesting, and commercial and recreational maritime pursuits.

City Dock to State Circle (bottom)

The view from the Annapolis Waterfront Hotel's rooftop includes intimate streets that fan out from Church Circle and State Circle, where the State House is the seat of government. George Washington admired the city's urban design so much that he had Pierre L'Enfant incorporate it into the nation's capital.

El Galeón Andalucía

A celebration of maritime craftsmanship, visiting ship *El Galeón Andalucía* is a replica of a 16th-century Spanish galleon. With masts more than 100 feet tall, the 496-ton ship cost some $5 million to build and is deemed to be the only galleon-class vessel sailing the world today.

Pride of Baltimore II *(above and left)*

Known in ports around the world, *Pride II* hosts some 100,000 visitors annually and is "Baltimore built" in the style of the city's War of 1812 topsail schooners. A waterfront museum, its mission is to promote historical maritime education, advance tourism, and represent the people of Maryland.

El Galeón Andalucía *(above and right)*

Constructed in 2009, *Andalucía* is a one-of-a-kind replica galleon class ship. Constructed of fiberglass and lined with wood, crews of between 15-35 people have manned her around the world visiting various ports and offering a glimpse into 16th-century maritime life.

L'Hermione (above and left)

L'Hermione is a replica of the 1779 French frigate that ferried the Marquis de Lafayette to the U.S. to aid American revolutionaries. Its maiden sail in 2015 was to Yorktown, Virginia. From there it called on more than a dozen ports along the east coast before arriving back in France.

Old Guard (opposite)

The U.S. Army Old Guard Fife and Drum Corps welcomed L'Hermione to the city of Annapolis. Created in 1960, the regiment marches in Colonial style red-coat uniforms, tricorn hats, and powdered wigs while playing patriotic music and performing precise drills.

Woodwind *(top and left)*

Locals and visitors alike delight in sailing from the decks of the twin 74-foot schooners, *Woodwind* and *Woodwind II*. The schooners set sail daily and offer breathtaking views of the port of Annapolis, Greenbury Point, the Chesapeake Bay Bridge, and beyond.

Wednesday Night Races

Since 1959, the Annapolis Yacht Club has hosted Wednesday Night Races. Today, more than 125 yachts compete in the midweek festivities in a variety of handicap and one-design classes.

Thomas Point Shoal Lighthouse

In 1877, ice plowed into this lighthouse causing a lantern to spill 200 gallons of oil. The keeper, a Civil War veteran, managed to escape in a rowboat. Today, visitors can explore his vigils through rough Chesapeake weather and automated technologies that make this lighthouse a NOAA weather station.

Annapolis Skyline *(top)*

A thriving shipping industry attracted great wealth to the colonial port of Annapolis and prosperous merchants built mansions, many with formal gardens and grand rooms for lavish entertaining. Today, Annapolis has more original 18th-century structures still standing than any other city in the United States.

Bay Bridge Fishing *(bottom)*

A diverse estuary that mingles fresh and salt waters, the Chesapeake Bay is home to more than 300 species of fish and numerous shellfish. Anglers have favorite spots to fish for striped bass, American eel, Atlantic menhaden, perch, and other species.

Bay Bridge Sunset *(pages 18–19)*

Ferries were the chief mode of transportation across the bay until the first span of the Bay Bridge, completed in 1952, connected Annapolis with Kent Island and the eastern shore. It is notably tall to accommodate shipping lanes for ocean-going vessels, historic tall ships, and tankers from around the world.

Wednesday Night Races (above)

Evening light illuminates a sailboat's spinnaker as the skipper sails toward the finish line on Spa Creek in front of the Annapolis Yacht Club. Wednesday Night Races begin in April and go through September and are a fun way to celebrate the mid-week.

Bay Bridge Spans (opposite)

The influx of travelers to the eastern shore led to the construction in 1973 of a three-lane second span of the Bay Bridge. Both bridges curve so that their main spans cross the bay's shipping channels at a 90-degree angle, as required by the U. S. Army Corps of Engineers.

Annapolis Harbor Moorings *(top)*

The "front forty" mooring fields between Spa Creek Bridge and the U.S. Naval Academy are the most popular of the city's many mooring fields. Sailors, like these U.S. Sailboat Show visitors, can stay here and hail a water taxi or motor a skiff to a town landing.

Miss Anne *(bottom)*

Passengers explore hidden gems along the shoreline of Spa Creek and Annapolis aboard *Miss Anne*. The snug launch offers tours that weave stories past and present about the city's intriguing people and events.

Chesapeake Buyboats

Wooden buyboats recall an era when oyster harvesting flourished on the bay. In the 1900s, buyboats transported produce and catch to market at ports on the Chesapeake Bay. Visitors can see classic wooden buyboats when they are moored at the maritime museums in Annapolis and St. Michaels.

Annapolis Harbor (above)

Thanks to the city's preservationists, visitors arriving by boat can view the Annapolis skyline as it has been seen for centuries: rows of 18th-century buildings punctuated by church steeples and the distinctive domes of the State House and U.S. Naval Academy.

Yacht Basin (opposite top)

Established in 1937, the Yacht Basin Company is Annapolis' oldest privately owned marina. It is home to 100 fixed slips and three deep-water slips that can accommodate vessels up to 240 feet. The annual slip-holder wait can take years given the basin is just steps from historic downtown and Eastport.

Harbor Queen (opposite bottom)

A familiar fixture at the end of City Dock, the 300-passenger *Harbor Queen* blasts her horn as she embarks on cruises on the Severn River and Chesapeake Bay. Passengers enjoy libations and narrated tours of the Annapolis' maritime history.

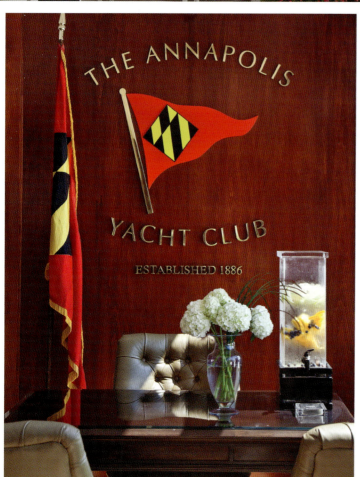

Annapolis Yacht Club (above and left)

The Annapolis Yacht Club began in 1886 as an informal canoe club and by 1888 a clubhouse for the "Severn Boat Club" was built on oyster shells at the foot of Duke of Gloucester Street. AYC launched Wednesday night and frostbite racing traditions and hosts international and North American events.

AYC Keel & Wheels
(opposite top and bottom)

Aficionados of classic cars and wooden boats display their collections, adorned with their AYC burgees, at the Annapolis Yacht Club. This annual autumn event is open to the public.

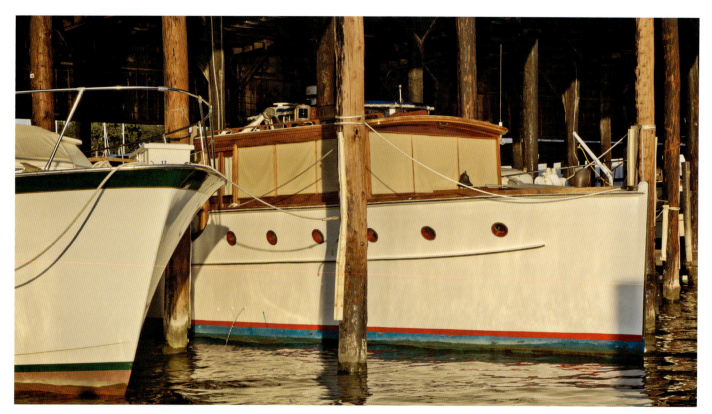

Spa Creek Covered Slips
(top and bottom)

Covered slips are a rarity in marinas and they occasionally dot the shorelines of Spa Creek and other waterways to protect boats from the elements. In its heyday, Sarles Boatyard and Marina, founded in 1907 on Spa Creek, included 21 covered slips and specialized in wooden boats.

SS Sophie (above and right)

After moving to Eastport in 1947, the legendary John Trumpy & Sons Inc. built several yachts before closing in 1973. The luxurious 80-foot SS Sophie is one of about 100 Trumpys that remain. Trumpys are prized for their craftsmanship, classic designs with elegant interiors, graceful bows, and flat sterns.

Kayakers on Spa Creek
(pages 30–31)

Paddling a kayak to town is a breeze in the quiet areas of Spa Creek. The lush grounds of the Charles Carroll House and St. Mary's Church slope down to one of the few remaining areas along the creek's shoreline that is free of piers and marinas.

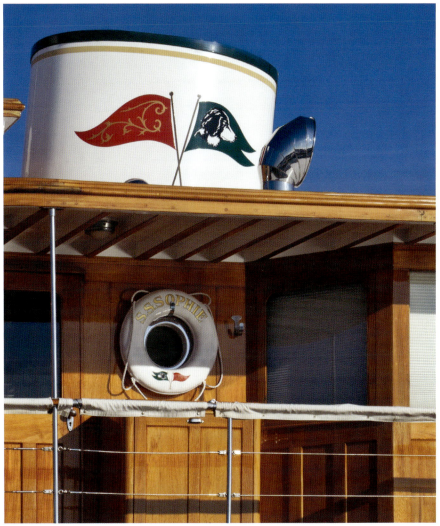

Stanley Norman at City Dock (above)

Each year some 3,000 students board the Chesapeake Bay Foundation's *Stanley Norman*, a floating classroom where they learn about Chesapeake watermen. Built in 1902, she is a single-masted sailing vessel designed to harvest oysters with a pair of dredges that are dragged across the bottom of the bay.

Main Street (opposite top and bottom)

At the foot of Main Street a French flag waves in honor of visiting ship *L'Hermione*. Lining the brick paved street are 18th- and 19th-century buildings that offer visitors a glimpse into Annapolis' history. The city has more than 1,500 historic structures dating from 1675 to 1930.

U.S. Naval Academy *(above and left)*

Established in 1845, the academy is situated on 338 acres on the former grounds of Fort Severn where the Severn River flows into Chesapeake Bay. Welcoming more than one million visitors annually, the campus is a blend of historic and modern buildings and features numerous monuments and memorials.

Bancroft Hall *(top)*

Midshipmen line up for lunchtime formation outside Bancroft Hall, considered the largest single dormitory in one building in the U.S. The Beaux-Arts structure has its own zip code, is home to the brigade of 4,000 midshipmen, and contains some 1,700 rooms and 4.8 miles of corridors.

USNA Sailing *(bottom)*

The Midshipmen receive training aboard these matching Navy 44s in ocean sailing, seamanship, navigation, leadership, and teamwork. The Naval Academy has the largest offshore sail training fleet for collegiate sailing in the United States and hosts many of intercollegiate sailing's big boat regattas.

Blue Angels

During Commissioning Week, the Blue Angels air show draws huge crowds to watch the Navy-trained pilots perform graceful, high-speed maneuvers, including the four-jet Diamond and the Delta formation. They fly above the Severn River, and viewing is best at Ingram Field, Farragut Field, and Hospital Point.

USNA Dress Parade *(above)*

The midshipmen present formal dress parades that are open to the public. On Worden Field, the brigade performs the manual of arms, renders honors to the senior officer or civilian dignitary present, and passes in review before the official party and guests.

U.S. Naval Academy Bridge
(pages 38–39)

The domes of the State House and U.S. Naval Academy come into view on the crest of this bridge over the Severn River. In 1994, the winning entry from a design competition replaced the former bascule bridge and was named in honor of the Naval Academy's 150th anniversary.

USNA Football *(top and bottom right)*

The U.S. Naval Academy football team played its first season in 1879, and today they are spirited competitors in the NCAA Division I conference. With decorated blue and gold horns, a live goat has been the team's mascot since 1893.

USNA- Marine Corps Stadium *(bottom left)*

This newly renovated facility is the home field of the Navy midshipmen football team, the men's lacrosse team, and the Chesapeake Bayhawks lacrosse team. Since 2013, it has also been the home of the college football Military Bowl and hosts a number of regional and international events.

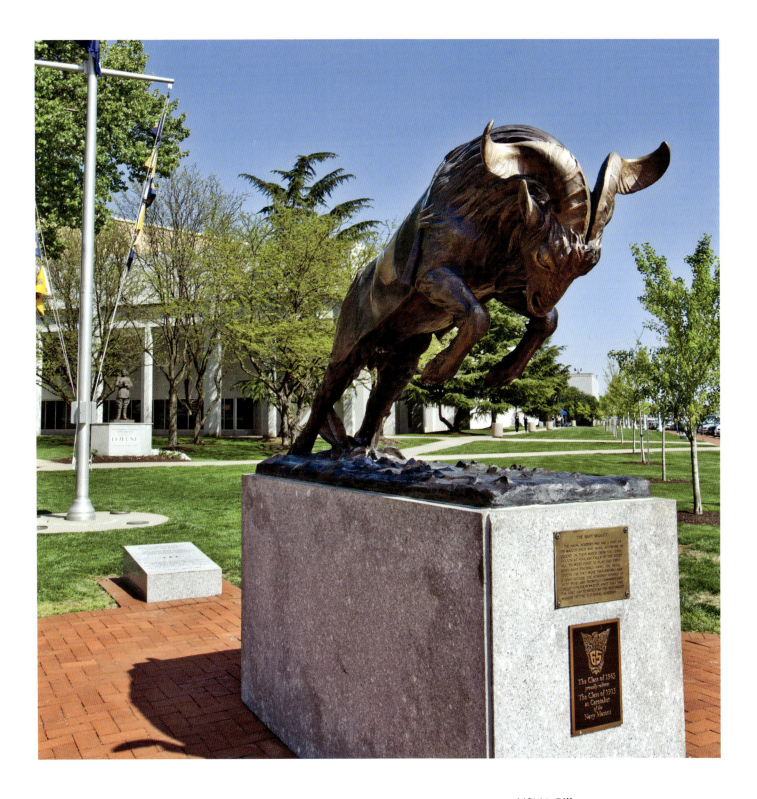

USNA Billy

Navy's fierce mascot, Bill the goat, leads the team's football rivalry with Army. As legend has it, in 1893 a live goat made its debut as a mascot at the fourth Army-Navy game when the USS *New York* dropped anchor off Annapolis and the ship's mascot came ashore.

Submarine Force Centennial

Sculptor Paul Wegner designed this bronze and marble memorial to commemorate 100 years of submarine usage by the United States Navy. Dedicated in 2000, the sculpture depicts a submarine breaching the surface during an emergency blow. Within the surrounding waves are human faces and dolphins.

Still on Patrol Monument *(above)*

A Mark XIV torpedo, a main armament of World War II submarines, honors the 374 officers and 3,131 men who lost their lives during World War II and are still on "patrol." The torpedo is cradled on a 15-foot blue granite base with the engraving, "Courage Runs Deep."

USNA Tecumseh *(right)*

Replicated from the figurehead of Native American chief Tamanend from the USS *Delaware*, which sunk in the Civil War, this statue was later renamed Tecumseh by the academy's midshipmen. Today, midshipmen cover him in war paint before competitions and throw pennies around the base for good luck during exam week.

USNA Officers Quarters *(top)*

Known as "Captains Row," these historical homes along Porter Road are for senior officers. Considered the most prestigious area in which to live, they were designed in 1905 by noted architect Ernest Flagg. Flagg, known for his Beaux Arts style, designed other USNA buildings such as the Chapel and Bancroft Hall.

USNA Chapel *(bottom and opposite)*

This Annapolis landmark has a noted pipe organ and Tiffany windows. Peter Marshall, pastor and future chaplain to the U.S. Senate, spoke here hours before the Japanese attack on Pearl Harbor. His sermon is credited in part for the class of 1942 graduating in 1941 to support the war.

USNA Model Ship Museum (above and opposite bottom)

The Class of 1951 Gallery of Ships is a collection of exquisitely crafted warship models from the 17th, 18th, and 19th centuries. In some cases, these models are the only complete surviving physical record of ships built during the classic Age of Sail.

USNA Bone Ship Models (opposite top)

These miniature ship models are a testament to the resilience of the human spirit. French prisoners of war incarcerated in England carved these ships mostly from the bones of their beef rations during the Anglo-French Wars of 1756-1815. The majority of these works were created during the Napoleonic Wars.

47

USNA Museum USS Constitution Exhibit *(opposite top)*

Located in Preble Hall, the museum showcases two floors of exhibits including ship models, paintings, uniforms, and more. This wooden model of "Old Ironsides" is a precisely crafted version of the legendary USS Constitution. Visitors can explore her 200-hundred-year history.

USNA Museum Civil War Exhibit *(opposite bottom)*

The museum brings the past to life for more than 100,000 visitors annually through vivid displays of every major American war, including this Civil War display. The exhibit highlights how important the Union and Confederate navies were to the outcome of the war.

USNA Museum Admiral Farragut *(above)*

Exhibited here is the long career of Admiral Farragut. Commissioned in the Navy in 1810 at age nine, he fought during the War of 1812 and the Civil War. In the midst of battle on the USS Hartford in 1864 he famously proclaimed, "Damn the torpedoes, full speed ahead!"

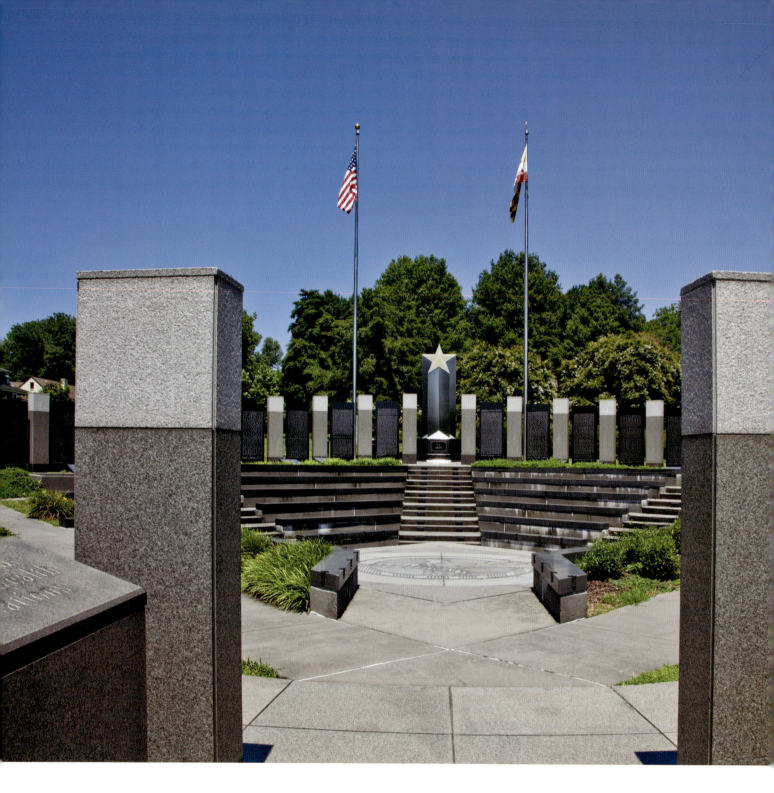

WWII Memorial

Overlooking the Severn River and the U.S. Naval Academy is an amphitheater with 48 pillars representing the 48 states at the time of World War II. The names of the more than 6,000 Marylanders who died in the war are inscribed on the memorial's columns and granite slabs.

Between Morning and Night
(top and bottom)

The Maryland Fire Rescue Memorial, *Between Morning and Night* by sculptor Rodney Carroll, honors the fallen and those who continue to selflessly serve. A firefighter and EMS provider ascend the "staircase of time" while figures reach out to console and say goodbye.

James Senate Office Building *(top)*

The William S. James Senate Office Building, renovated in 2001-2002, is home to 35 Maryland state senators and restored ceremonial rooms that are used to host dignitaries. Two of the rooms hold silver candelabra chandeliers from the 1930s. The splendid Victorian fountain is on the grounds of the Governor's House.

Chief Justice Taney

A statue of Roger B. Taney, Chief Justice of the Supreme Court, honors the Marylander who is known for casting the 1857 decisive vote in the *Dred Scott* decision, which denied African-Americans the rights of citizenship. This statue teaches an important lesson in history.

53

Maryland State House
(above and right)

An iconic Annapolis landmark, this is the oldest state capitol still in continuous legislative use and is the only state house to have served as the nation's Capitol. During that time, George Washington resigned as commander-in-chief of the Continental Army and the Treaty of Paris was ratified, ending the Revolutionary War.

Capital Dome *(opposite)*

Annapolis architect Joseph Clark designed what is today the largest wooden dome of its kind in the U.S. Completed in 1794, it is held together by wooden pegs. The "Franklin" lightening rod, constructed and grounded to Benjamin Franklin's specifications, is seen by some as an expression of the young nation's ingenuity and independence.

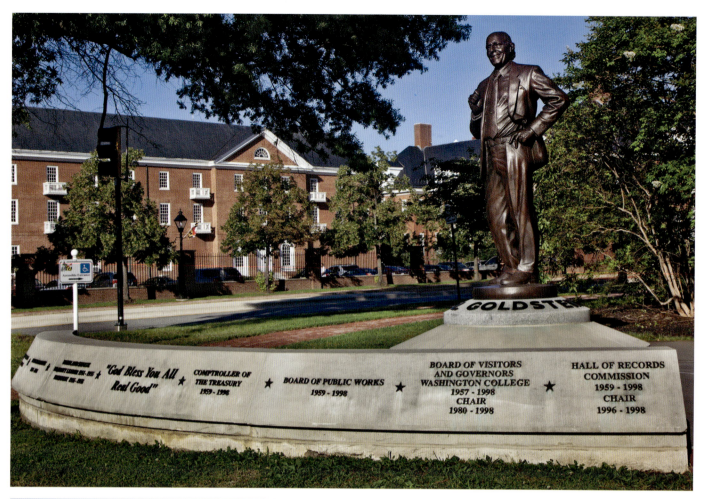

Louis Goldstein (above)

One of the longest-serving state officials in U.S. history, this legendary politician and comptroller of Maryland served for 40 years. At the time of his death in 1998, he became Maryland's first elected official to lie in state under the State House Rotunda.

Water Witch (left)

In colonial times, firefighting was every citizen's duty. By 1839, the city's first volunteer fire department was formed. By 1886, the Annapolis Water Witch Hook & Ladder Company was built. The existing 1913 historic structure is the second firehouse at this location.

State House Grounds (opposite)

From the city's highest land, the view of brick-lined streets radiating from State Circle to Main Street and City Dock is spectacular. The grounds are home to the Old Treasury and several historic memorials.

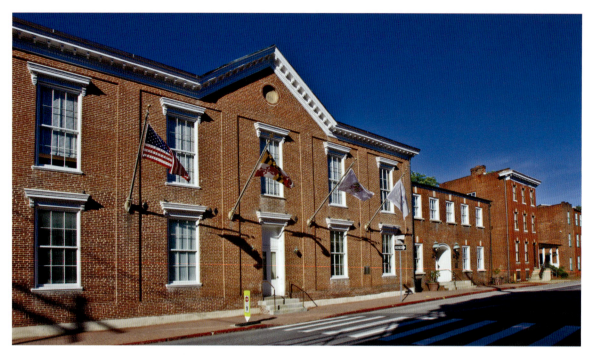

City Hall (top)

Assembly rooms, circa 1760s, burned during the Civil War after being taken over by Union troops. Today, City Hall's Italianate structure includes surviving walls of the original assembly rooms. This National Historic Landmark is home to the Mayor's office, City Council Chambers, and changing art exhibitions.

Old Treasury Building (bottom)

Located on the grounds of the State House, the Old Treasury, circa 1735–36, is the oldest public building in Annapolis. This one-story Flemish bond brick structure was built to serve the office of the Commissioners and only later was it used as a treasury.

Treasury Building (opposite)

Named after Comptroller of the Treasury Louis L. Goldstein, this is the home of the Treasurer's office. In Maryland, the Treasurer is elected by a joint ballot of both houses of the General Assembly, a tradition begun following the Constitutional Convention of 1851, at which the Board of Public Works was created.

Lawyers Mall (opposite top)

Marylanders often rally for the causes they care about at Lawyers Mall—also called State House Square—especially during the legislative session. Today's state legislators meet for 90 days each year to act on more than 2,300 bills affecting Marylanders.

Old Post Office (opposite bottom)

Since 1901, Annapolitans have been posting letters and socializing at the Old Post Office building on Church Circle, steps from the State House, Governor's Mansion, and St. Anne's church. The post office has closed but the Georgian Revival-style building, purchased by the state, survives.

Justice Marshall (above)

A statue of Baltimore-born Thurgood Marshall, the first African-American Justice of the U.S. Supreme Court, is steps from the former site of the court building. Here, the young attorney argued discrimination cases leading to his victory with *Brown v. Board of Education*, a decision that desegregated public schools.

State Circle (above)

One of two circles in historic Annapolis, intimate brick-lined streets radiate from State Circle, a confluence of activity that includes the seat of the legislature and bustling shops. This well-preserved, photogenic area has often been cordoned off for camera crews filming major motion pictures.

Robert Johnson House (left)

Annapolis is notable for its abundance of Georgian-style homes. The land beneath this house once belonged to an Annapolis barber, Robert Johnson. In 1773, Johnson's grandson built this Georgian-style brick home at 23 State Circle. Today, it is one of several boutique historic inns in downtown Annapolis.

Governor Calvert House

This 51-room historic inn, festooned with holiday greens, was the home of two former Maryland governors and the site of an archeological dig in the 1980s and early 1990s. Historic Annapolis Inc., the National Endowment for the Humanities, and other institutions financed the excavation of the Calvert House.

Government House Conservatory (above)

There are seven public rooms in the Government House and each plays an important role as the Governor and his family greet guests from around the world: the Entrance Hall, the Conservatory, the Victorian Library, the Reception Room, the Parlor, the Drawing Room, and the State Dining Room.

Government House Parlor (left)

The elegant parlor of this Georgian style home features the Thomas Johnson clock by well-known cabinetmaker, John Fessler. Johnson was Maryland's first governor. Some of the notable guests to the mansion in the past have included Mark Twain, Queen Elizabeth, and Sugar Ray Leonard.

Government House (above)

This home of Maryland Governors since 1870 is alive with historic furnishings, paintings, and works of art from around the world. A portrait by Charles Wilson Peale of George Washington hangs in the Drawing Room. There are furnishings by Potthast, eminent 19th-century Baltimore furniture makers, and Peabody Art Collection works.

Government House Dining Room (right)

The State Dining Room, a gracious setting for distinguished guests, features a portrait of the Governor Horatio Sharpe and his family, circa 1754, by Gawen Hamilton. Sharpe was provincial governor of Maryland from 1753 to 1768.

Maynard-Burgess (top)

The Maynard-Burgess House was continuously owned by African-Americans from about 1850 to 1980—a timeframe spanning slavery, the Civil War, and the Civil Rights Movement. Born a free African-American, John Maynard purchased and freed his wife, her daughter, and mother-in-law between 1834 and 1845.

Peggy Stewart House (bottom)

In 1774, merchant Anthony Stewart made the mistake of paying the British tax on a cargo of tea. Angry citizens forced him to burn his ship, the *Peggy Stewart*, which was named after his daughter. The event later became known as the "Annapolis Tea Party." His Georgian style house was nicknamed after his ship.

Museum Store (above)

Rebuilt after fire damaged much of this block in 1790, merchants set up shop in this former bakery. Today, the shop features wares inspired by the Chesapeake region. Proceeds from purchases support the Historic Annapolis Foundation and its mission to preserve Annapolis for future generations.

Brice House (right)

James Brice, an aide-de-camp of George Washington during the American Revolution, had this elegant five-part plan home built in the Georgian style between 1767 and 1773. Built for entertaining in town, some called it a "town home." It is one of the most well-preserved colonial homes in the country.

Paca Garden *(above)*

The two-acre garden, restored to its original splendor, is an exquisite refuge with a summer house, native and heirloom plants, and an urban kitchen garden. The brick walls enclose formal parterres characteristic of colonial gardens in the Chesapeake region. The Paca House and Gardens is a National Historic Landmark.

Paca House Bed Chamber *(left)*

The Paca House and Gardens, circa 1763-1765, welcomes visitors into the 18th-century life of lawyer and patriot William Paca. Guests can see a restored one-story office and kitchen pavilions, and their connecting hyphens, public and private quarters, and behind the-scenes operations of the mansion.

William Paca House *(above and right)*

William Paca, a patriot, signatory of the Declaration of Independence, and a three-term governor of Maryland, designed much of his Georgian mansion. It is a grand example of a five-part Palladian-plan house. On its upper floor, the Paca family could view the garden, entertain guests, and enjoy cool breezes.

Waterfront Warehouse
(above and left)

On Pinkney Street is a rare surviving example of the small warehouses that dotted the Annapolis waterfront in the 18th and early 19th centuries. Tobacco growers brought their crops to merchants' warehouses to be inspected and stored until a large enough cargo was ready to ship to England.

Shiplap (above and right)

The Shiplap House, circa 1715, was a tavern and shop in the 18th century. One of the oldest surviving houses in historic Annapolis, it is named for shiplap—the random-width flush wooden boards used as siding on its rear façade. The large, wide planks were likely hewn from mature trees.

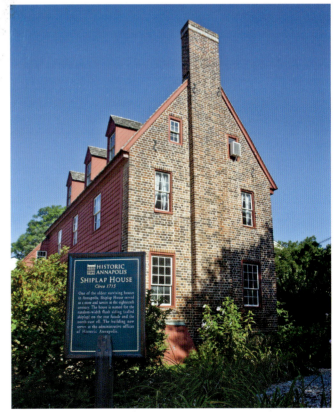

Hammond Harwood House
(opposite, top and bottom)

This National Historic Landmark is a striking five-part Anglo-Palladian design. It features furniture by cabinetmaker John Shaw, including an elegant sideboard, an original Harwood family piece, and a tall clock. Paintings by Charles Wilson Peale are original to the house.

Hammond Harwood House *(above)*

This exquisite structure, circa 1774, is one of architect William Buckland's masterpieces. It features some of the nation's finest woodcarving and plasterwork. Its Doric-order arched entryway has perfectly proportioned columns and pilasters. Much of Annapolis' Georgian splendor is attributed to Buckland's influence.

Hogshead *(above)*

This early 19th-century gambrel-roofed building is similar to the frame structures that housed many colonial Annapolis families and served as barracks for new military recruits during the Revolutionary War. Most of these men stayed only a few days or weeks before shipping out.

Hogshead's Modest Interiors
(opposite top and bottom)

Through an interactive experience, colonial reenactors dramatize the daily life of the lower and middle classes in early Maryland. This one-and-a-half-story frame house rests on a brick foundation typical of modest 18th-century dwellings.

Banneker-Douglass Museum (above)

Named for Benjamin Banneker and Frederick Douglass, this distinctive museum is dedicated to preserving Maryland's African-American heritage. It is housed in the historic Mt. Moriah A.M.E Church, which served as the meeting hall for the first African Methodist Episcopal Church, originally formed in the 1790s.

Chase Lloyd House (left)

This three-story Georgian mansion, circa 1769–1774, has a beautiful staircase with floating treads cantilevered from adjacent walls. It was built for Samuel Chase, a Declaration of Independence signatory and an Associate Justice of the Supreme Court. The main floor and gardens are open for tours.

St. Anne's Parish *(above and right)*

St. Anne's Parish was the only church in colonial Annapolis, aside from a private chapel for Roman-Catholics in Charles Carroll of Carrollton's home. Today's church was built in the Romanesque Revival style after an 1858 fire. A stained-glass window by Tiffany Studios shows St. Anne with the Blessed Virgin Mary.

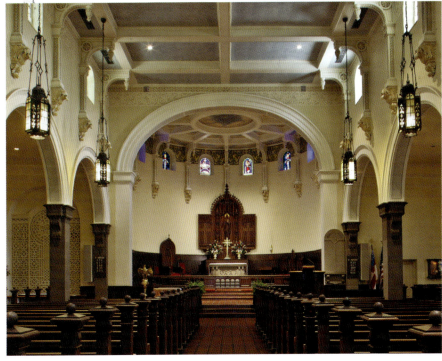

Charles Carroll House and St. Mary's *(above and opposite)*

Once the seat of the Catholic Carrolls of Annapolis, this was the home of Charles Carroll, the only Catholic signer of the Declaration of Independence. His heirs donated the land for St. Mary's Church to the Redemptorists. The church, circa 1858–1860, has a Gothic high altar, exquisite frescoes, and stained-glass windows.

Reynolds Tavern *(left)*

William Reynolds, a hatter and tavern keeper, built this structure in 1737, which later became a tavern. Its beautiful entrance porch dates back to 1812 and was the work of prominent cabinetmaker John Shaw. Located on Church Circle, the tavern's colonial ambiance makes for a special dining experience.

Historic London Town and Gardens (top)

Located just 18 miles from Annapolis, London Town was created in 1683 by the Maryland legislature and soon became a major tobacco port in the colonial trans-Atlantic trade network. Colonial militia fire a volley from their muskets aimed at the South River.

William Brown House (bottom)

By the 1720s, London Town rivaled Annapolis as a transportation and trade center. The port teamed with industry as merchants, planters, carpenters, and coopers were important to the tobacco trade. With dramatic views of the South River, the William Brown House is one of two buildings from colonial London Town.

Lord Mayor's Tenement (top)

Named for self-proclaimed Mayor of London Town David Mackelfish, this reconstructed tenement house dates back to the early 1700s. Although none of the original tenement dwellings survived, it is believed that ninety-five percent of colonial Marylanders lived in small dwellings like the Lord Mayor's Tenement.

London Town Militia (bottom)

The colonial militia re-enactment is an annual event that includes musket fire and cannons. Visitors see firsthand the roles the militia played during colonial times and experience living history at London Town by exploring the grounds and buildings.

Quiet Waters Sculpture

At Quiet Waters, native plants, bridges, gazebos and outdoor sculptures, such as *Blue Herons in Flight*, offer a serene retreat. The Native Plant Garden near the Blue Heron Center is full of seasonal delights, with fountains in warm weather and an ice rink in the winter.

Quiet Waters

Annapolitans hike, bike, and paddle this 340-acre oasis between the South River and Harness Creek with more than six miles of trails, scenic overlooks, and picnic pavilions along its wooded shoreline. The park hosts outdoor concerts, art festivals, boat rentals, and a dog park that is popular on Sunday mornings.

St. John's Bell (opposite top)

In 1950 the U.S. Treasury Department cast in copper 48 reproductions of the Philadelphia Liberty Bell. This replica on the front lawn of St. John's College celebrates the founding fathers' "principles of freedom." The pediment for the bell was erected with the pennies donated by the children of Anne Arundel County.

St. John's vs. USNA (opposite bottom)

The Annapolis Cup, an annual croquet match that pits the Midshipmen against the Johnnies, is a cherished rite of spring. Spectators in Great Gatsby-style attire host champagne picnics during this spirited rivalry. Each year the midshipmen wear croquet whites and the Johnnies unveil surprise uniforms.

St. John's College (above)

Founded as King Williams School in 1696, St. John's is a liberal arts college located in downtown Annapolis. Known for its distinctive curriculum, Francis Scott Key, who penned the National Anthem, is one of many of its prominent alumni.

May Day Businesses *(left and right)*

The May Day tradition of displaying floral arrangements on windows, porches, and doors began as a Garden Club of Old Annapolis Towne beautification project in 1956. Today, residents and business owners compete for winning ribbons and an invitation to the Garden Club's Annual Tea.

May Day State Circle

Harry Brown's, an Annapolis icon, welcomes patrons with flowers and wine. For more than 50 years Annapolitans have decorated the doors of historic shops and homes for May Day with artful fresh-cut arrangements and ribbon-laced flowers.

May Day Maryland Avenue

(left and right)

On May Day, judges from the City's Garden Club stroll the historic district and Murray Hill neighborhoods to award winners in many categories. To be considered in the judging, all baskets must be hung by 10 a.m.

May Day at Helly Hansen

Adirondack chairs and a festive red bike beckon pedestrians to pause and take in the fragrant May Day flowers and sparkling skies on Main Street. This storefront is hoping to earn a coveted winning ribbon.

McGarvey's Saloon (above)

A long-time community gathering place, patrons savor tidewater specialties, including fresh oysters and Maryland crab soup, at this saloon that neighbors historic colonial taverns that line Market Space.

Westgate Circle (left)

The Annapolis Art in Public Places Commission selected Bobby Donovan's sculpture *Shoals* for this gateway circle in Annapolis' Arts District. Many describe it as fish swimming above the ribs of a sunken ship. Constructed of oak, this artwork pays homage to the city's maritime roots.

Ram's Head On Stage (above)

Located next to the Ram's Head Tavern, the Muehlhauser family purchased the historic site in 1989. Today, some of the country's finest musicians perform in this intimate venue where patrons enjoy dining while listening to headliner acts.

Ram's Head Tavern (right)

Since the late 1700s, patrons have gathered at Ram's Head for pub food and drink. In the 18th century, it was called "The Crown and Dial" and "Sign of the Green Tree." Today, the pub is known for its selection of beers, dog friendly café, and live music.

Visitors Center (top)

A red plaque identifies this structure as 18th-century vernacular, a perfect setting from which visitors can discover Annapolis. Located in the heart of the historic district, this is "Grand Central" for tours. A satellite visitor information booth at City Dock is open from March through October.

King George Street Residence (opposite)

This private residence nestled on the corner of King George and East streets has a bronze plaque, which signifies an 18th-century building of national importance. The Historic Marker Program highlights more than 240 properties of the historic district.

May Day Doors
(above, left, and opposite)

The doors of Annapolis are awash in color on May Day with whimsical and inventive floral arrangements and brightly colored ribbon-laced baskets. Rain or shine, Annapolitans regard May Day as one of the city's most beautiful days and a welcomed tradition.

Flag House B&B

Steps from the City Dock and Gate 1 of the U.S. Naval Academy, this intimate inn offers a personal touch. Upon arrival, guests are welcomed by their state or national flag flying from the porch. Originally two Victorian townhouses, this 1870 home was restored in the 1990s and is known for its ambiance.

Cantler's (above)

Once a well-kept secret, word has gotten out about Cantler's fresh seafood and tranquil setting where diners arrive by car or boat, or even on foot, to walk the docks and peek at peelers in floats on Mill Creek. The Cantler family has worked in the seafood industry for five generations.

Chez Amie B&B (right)

With architectural roots dating to the late 1800s, this little gem of an inn is located in the heart of the city's downtown. Before becoming a B&B, it served the Fleet and East Street neighborhoods as Sam's Brothers Groceries store from the early 1900s through 1970s.

Gibson's Lodging (above)

In 1681, this building was assigned to the First Naval Officer of the Port of Annapolis. The original structure, called "The Old Courthouse," burned in 1691. The existing 18th-century Georgian-style home was renovated in 1905 and in 1980, Gibson's Lodging opened as an inn.

Georgian House B&B (left)

Annapolis is unique in the large number of Georgian homes in the historic district, many with distinctive brickwork. This B&B proudly displays a basket of flowers and ribbons for May Day.

Zimmerman Wilson House (opposite)

Charles Zimmerman, U.S. Naval Academy bandmaster and choir director from 1887–1916, ordered this ornate Queen Anne style house with spindle work and fish-scale shingles from a mail order catalogue. In 1906, as organist at St. Mary's Church, he composed the music for the Navy song, *Anchors Aweigh*.

Annapolis City Marina

A familiar landmark for boaters and landlubbers, the Annapolis City Marina is a popular water taxi stop, connecting City Dock and Eastport. Boaters find refuge at the full-service fuel dock and more than 80 fixed-pier, in-water slips.

East Street

Annapolis has more colonial structures than any other location in the country. Color-coded plaques on historically significant buildings lead visitors through centuries of architecture and preservation. These plaques, along with American, Maryland, and Naval Academy flags, are seen throughout the city.

Aerial of Annapolis

While shipping trade and commerce eventually shifted to the deeper harbor in Baltimore, Annapolis has grown as an international center for recreational and competitive boating, with world-class racing, boat shows, and nautical services.

Liberté *(above and right)*

The 77-foot *Liberté* schooner is privately owned and based on Spa Creek and Cape Cod, Massachusetts. Available for private themed charters, this two-masted gaff-rigged schooner is intended as a heavy but fast offshore cruiser.

103

Maritime Museum's Lighthouse

The Annapolis Maritime Museum offers educational programs that explore the ecology and maritime history of the Chesapeake Bay. It is one of four partners in a consortium that owns the Thomas Point Shoal Lighthouse, and its tours offer a rare glimpse of the keeper's life at this offshore beacon.

Annapolis Maritime Museum

Recently renovated, this museum is at the site of McNasby Oyster Co., on Back Creek, near marinas, sailmakers, yacht designers, boat brokers, and chandleries. It celebrates the Chesapeake's maritime heritage with exhibits and lectures, community events, concerts, art shows, and educational programs.

Spa Creek Bridge

Connecting Annapolis with Eastport, this bascule bridge only has a 17 foot clearance, thus requiring its keeper to draw it open about 3,800 times a year. Spa Creek is the main thoroughfare to the city's neighborhoods for all boaters.

Osprey (above)

Nesting ospreys on channel markers and pilings are one of the first signs of spring on the Chesapeake Bay. While feeding almost exclusively on fish, these large raptors grow up to 2 feet in length and can have a wingspan of up to 6 feet.

Blue Heron (right)

The great blue heron is a slender wading bird with a graceful bill and neck. It can be seen year-round throughout the Chesapeake Bay region, along the shoreline, riprap, and in wetlands—often silently hunting for food.

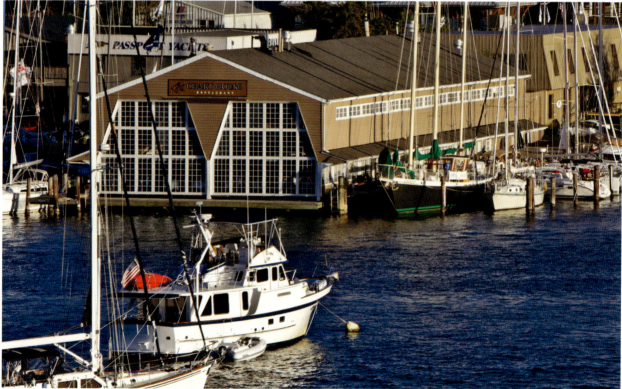

Wednesday Night Races *(top)*

The Annapolis Yacht Club's Wednesday Night Races, a summer tradition since 1960, draw spectators to the club, the nearby Spa Creek drawbridge, and to City Dock's bars and restaurants. Skippers navigate the harbor's mooring fields before crossing the finish line.

Chart House *(bottom)*

Eastport's maritime history includes the Annapolis Yacht Yard, which built torpedo boats during World War II, and Trumpy Yacht Yard, which built presidential yachts like the USS *Sequoia*. Today, the former Trumpy's is the Chart House restaurant where patrons enjoy harbor views, boat races, and the EYC Parade of Lights.

Boatyard Bar and Grill *(top)*

An environmental steward of the Chesapeake, the Boatyard is a member of One Percent for The Planet, a group of businesses who donate more than one percent of their annual sales to environmental preservation. The Boatyard has received the Annapolis Environmental Stewardship Certification.

Boatyard Mural *(bottom)*

Local artist Cindy Fletcher created two murals along Fourth Street in Eastport. The owner of the Boatyard Bar and Grill commissioned this work in 2013 and the Eastport Civic Association commissioned the other mural, *Great Wall of Eastport*, which was the first in the city.

Eastport Yacht Club

With spectacular views of the Bay Bridge, Greenbury Point, Annapolis Harbor, and the U.S. Naval Academy, the Eastport Yacht Club was founded in 1985. Today, it is a community-gathering place full of activity on and off shore, including championship regattas, a junior sailing program, charity events, and cruising.

Severn Sailing Association
(top and bottom)

For more than 50 years SSA, located on Annapolis Harbor, has hosted major regional, national, and international championship sailing events. SSA offers an active junior sailing program, a spring through fall season of racing, and a winter frostbiting series.

Sock Burn Oyster Roast (above)

Annapolitans celebrate spring and the start of the boating season with a ceremonial sock burning event. As legend has it, a local boat builder invited colleagues to join him as he lit his socks on fire. After he moved in 1994, the Eastport Yacht Club and Annapolis Maritime Museum continued the tradition.

Pirate Adventures (opposite)

Notorious pirates roamed the Chesapeake in the 17th century. Today, piracy is fun and this adventure boat delights children with the magic of searching for buried treasure. With a mischievous crew, children learn about maps, discover a message in a bottle, and more. The ship sails daily from Eastport during the summer.

Eastport Tug of War *(above and left)*

This enduring rivalry between the Maritime Republic of Eastport and the citizens from the other side of Spa Creek is an annual rite of autumn that benefits local charities. Warrior teams from pubs and taverns from both sides of the creek compete for a coveted trophy.

Memorial Day Parade *(top and bottom)*

Annapolis honors members of the military who have given their lives serving their country with a host of events, including an annual parade beginning on Amos Garrett Boulevard, traveling along West Street, Church Circle, then down Main Street to the Market House.

Whitehall Bay

Boaters on this scenic bay near the Bay Bridge and Sandy Point, a few miles from downtown Annapolis, often raft-up with fellow cruisers or explore by boat sites, such as the lovely Whitehall Manor house, circa 1764, located on the peninsula between Whitehall Creek and Meredith Creek.

Sandy Point (above)

Beachgoers at this state park view the panorama of ocean-going tankers, recreational anglers, and the daily stream of vehicles that cross the Chesapeake Bay Bridge. Sandy Point State Park, the last exit before the bridge toll, hosts the Maryland Seafood Festival, Bay Blues Festival, Lights on the Bay, and the Polar Bear Plunge.

Back Creek (pages 118–119)

Early birds savor the peaceful quiet of a sunrise on Back Creek. By late morning the creek will be busy as boaters cruise into eclectic Eastport, where original cottages are perched next to refined residences, maritime enterprises, and the occasional live-a-board moored at one of the many marinas.

Wednesday Night Races

A-2 Class sailboats unfurl their spinnakers as they head downwind. Spectator boats follow racers after the start, and then head back to watch the finish in front of the AYC clubhouse, where skippers and crew gather for a post-race party at the club.

Annapolis Newport Race

The 475-mile biennial Annapolis-Newport race connects two historic seaports on a route that includes the Chesapeake Bay, one of the nation's largest estuaries, and the Atlantic Ocean. Two Navy skippers—the sails are easy to spot—join the race.

Schooner Race

Schooners hauled cargo on the bay, competing for the best prices by beating others to the ports of Baltimore and Portsmouth/Norfolk. Their historic rivalry is rekindled each autumn during the Chesapeake Bay Schooner Race, which starts south of the Bay Bridge near Annapolis.

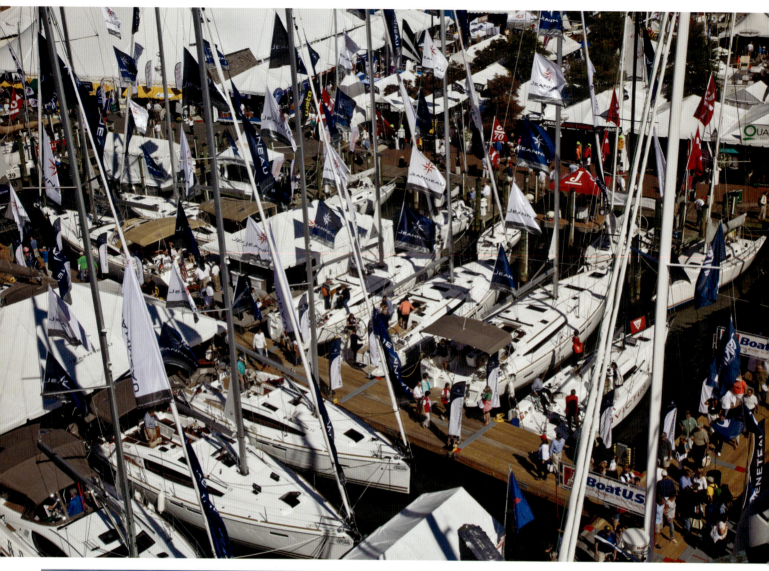

U.S. Sailboat Show *(above and left)*

In October, sailors convene on extensive display docks for the largest and oldest in-water sailboat show in the world. Visitors can board most new models on the market, make side-by-side comparisons, and explore navigational equipment, high-tech electronics, boating accessories, and nautical services.

U.S. Powerboat Show
(above and right)

For more than 40 years, boaters have attended the oldest in-water powerboat show in the world at City Dock. Exhibits range from luxurious motor and ocean-going yachts and "down east" trawlers to high-performance powerboats and offshore fishing vessels.

EYC Light Parade (top and bottom)

Spectators and skippers join the jolly revelry on the second Saturday in December as dozens of sailboats and powerboats illuminate the night, cruising on Spa Creek decked out in holiday light displays. The Eastport Yacht Club Light Parade is a signature Annapolis event.

Fireworks (opposite)

Boaters moor in Annapolis Harbor and pedestrians line piers from the Eastport Yacht Club to Spa Creek Bridge to watch Independence Day fireworks. The city takes great pride in its patriotic display and delights onlookers again with fireworks on New Year's Eve.

Lisa Masson is an award-winning commercial and fine art photographer with a wide range of experience, from international location shoots to diverse studio work. Since 1986, her clients have included upscale hotels, architectural firms, noted interior designers, magazines, and advertising agencies. Lisa's fine art photography appears in hotels, numerous private collections, and at her gallery in Eastport. Since the early days of her career in a small studio on Capitol Hill in Washington, D.C., Lisa has created compelling images with dramatic lighting. After spending 10 years working out of her 3,000 square-foot studio in Arlington, Va., Lisa discovered sailing, the Chesapeake Bay and moved to Annapolis. In addition to creating stylistic images for her commercial clients, she has been photographing Annapolis and its hidden gems ever since. Her fine art photography, displayed at Lisa Masson Studio Gallery on Fourth Street, features her original museum-quality imagery. To learn more about Lisa's work please visit www.LisaMassonPhotography.com

Annapolis native **Patricia Dempsey** is a seasoned communications professional with a flair for storytelling. She has extensive experience as a journalist, media relations director, and editorial consultant and works closely with authors, photographers, and subject matter specialists. As a regular contributor to the Washington Post Magazine, she interviewed intriguing, well-known subjects about their work and authored travel essays on destinations near and far. Her feature on Chesapeake lighthouses remains especially popular. A former "Traveling Gourmet" columnist and magazine editor, she criss-crossed the region to showcase Chesapeake culture, places, and people.

Her stories have also appeared in national publications such as More magazine. She has a master's degree from Johns Hopkins University and is a member of the American Society of Authors and Journalists.